© 2004 by Barbour Publishing, Inc.

ISBN 1-59310-001-9

Cover image © PhotoDisc

Scripture quotations marked NIV are taken from the HOLY BIBLE, NEW INTERNATIONAL VERSION®. NIV®. Copyright © 1973, 1978, 1984 by International Bible Society. Used by permission of Zondervan Publishing House. All rights reserved.

Scripture quotations marked NLT are taken from the *Holy Bible*, New Living Translation, copyright © 1996. Used by permission of Tyndale House Publishers, Inc. Wheaton, Illinois 60189, U.S.A. All rights reserved.

Published by Humble Creek, P.O. Box 719, Uhrichsville, Ohio 44683

Printed in China.
5 4 3 2 1

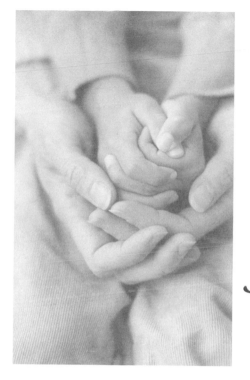

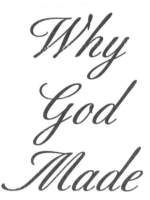

Why God Made Mothers

Larissa Carrick

HUMBLECREEK
INSPIRATION FOR LIFE

Why God Made Mothers

She is worth more than precious rubies.

PROVERBS 31:10 NLT

Mothers are our past.
The lines I see in my face are that of my mother,
and her mother, and her mother as well.

Mothers are our present.
They are the living embodiment of love—raising
and training children for the future.

Mothers are our future.
They keep us moving on, growing, striving to be
more like Christ, loving us unconditionally. . . .

Why God Made Mothers

Why did God make mothers?
To teach us how to love Him.
To teach us how to love.

Family faces are magic mirrors.
Looking at people who belong to us,
we see the past, present, and future.

GAIL LUMET BUCKLEY

Heirlooms we don't have in our family.
But stories we've got.

ROSE CHERNIN

My Mother

Who ran to help me when I fell,
And would some pretty story tell,
Or kiss the place to make it well?
My Mother.

JANE TAYLOR

Why God Made Mothers

Motherhood:

All love begins and ends there.

ROBERT BROWNING

A mother is a friend,
an example,
a stronghold, never failing. . . .

A mother is the truest friend we have, when trials, heavy and sudden, fall upon us; when adversity takes the place of prosperity, when friends who rejoice with us in our sunshine desert us when troubles thicken around us; still will she cling to us, and endeavor by her kind precepts and counsel to dissipate the clouds of darkness, and cause peace to return to our hearts.

WASHINGTON IRVING

Mothers Are a Blessing

She is clothed with strength and dignity.

PROVERBS 31:25 NLT

*God must love me
very much to have blessed me
with you as my mom.*

All that I am or hope to be I owe to my angel mother.
I remember my mother's prayers and
they have always followed me.
They have clung to me all my life.

ABRAHAM LINCOLN

Pride is one of the seven deadly sins;
but it cannot be the pride of
a mother in her children,
for that is compound of two cardinal virtues—
faith and hope.

CHARLES DICKENS

Most of the stones for the buildings of the City of God,
and all the best of them, are made by mothers.

HENRY DRUMMOND

When you thought I wasn't looking, I saw you hang my first painting on the refrigerator, and I wanted to paint another one. When you thought I wasn't looking, I saw you feed a stray cat, and I thought it was good to be kind to animals. When you thought I wasn't looking, I saw you make my favorite cake for me, and I knew that little things are special things. When you thought I wasn't looking, I heard you pray, and I believed there is a God I could always talk to. When you thought I wasn't looking, I felt you kiss me good night, and I felt loved. When you thought I wasn't looking, I saw tears come from your eyes, and I learned that sometimes things hurt, but it's all right to cry. When you thought I wasn't looking, I saw you give to someone needy and I learned the joy of giving. When you thought I wasn't looking, I saw you always did your best and it made me want to be all that I could be. When you thought I wasn't looking, I heard you say "thank you" and I wanted to say thanks for all the things I saw when you thought I wasn't looking.

AUTHOR UNKNOWN

Father,

You have showered me with blessings. You have given me the strength to sustain my family in times of trouble. You have filled my heart with Your peace when I have forgotten it. You have seen us through the difficult times, never ceasing in the lessons You teach us to better our lives and lead us to Your kingdom. You have filled our hearts with love, have given us what we need to live fully, and have often blessed us with more than we need. Thank You for my loving family. I pray that You will continue to bless us with Your Word, Your presence, and Your promise. I ask these things in the name of Your Son. Amen.

Why God Made Mothers

Mothers Teach Us Well

She sets about her work vigorously;
her arms are strong for her tasks.
PROVERBS 31:17 NIV

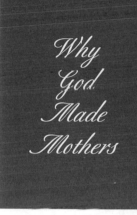

Why God Made Mothers

The mother's heart is the child's schoolroom.
HENRY WARD BEECHER

You train a child until age ten.
After that, you only influence them.
AUTHOR UNKNOWN

The great academy, a mother's knee.
THOMAS CARLYLE

You have taught me well. . . .

The older women. . .
can train the younger women to
love their husbands and children,
to be self-controlled and pure,
to be busy at home, to be kind.

TITUS 2:3–5 NIV

Keep reminding them of these things.

2 TIMOTHY 2:14 NIV

There is only one way to bring up a child
in the way that he should go
and that is to travel that way yourself.

ABRAHAM LINCOLN

Why
God
Made
Mothers

Children miss nothing in sizing up their parents.
If you are only half convinced of your beliefs,
they will quickly discern that fact.

JAMES DOBSON

The successful mother, the mother who does her part
in rearing and training aright the boys and girls
who are to be the men and women of the next generation,
is of greater use to the community. . . .
She is more important by far than the successful statesman
or businessman or artist or scientist.

THEODORE ROOSEVELT

My sainted mother taught me a devotion to God
and a love to country which have ever sustained me
in my many lonely and bitter moments of decision
in distant and hostile lands.
To her, I yield anew a son's reverent thanks.

GENERAL DOUGLAS MACARTHUR

*Training a child
to follow Christ
is easy for parents;
all they have to do
is lead the way.*

AUTHOR UNKNOWN

You have omitted to mention the greatest of my teachers—
my mother.

WINSTON CHURCHILL,
on being asked to check a list
of those who had taught him

Give a man a fish and he will eat for a day;
teach him how to fish and he will eat forever.

AUTHOR UNKNOWN

One should not only serve youth but should also
avoid offending them by word or deed.
One should give them the best of training
that they may learn to pray.

MARTIN LUTHER

Mom,

I don't know if you will ever understand how much you have taught me. I know I was not always easy to teach. I didn't always listen. I didn't always care to try. Sometimes I even thought that I knew better than you did. Forgive me for my ignorance. Deep down I always knew that you had my best interest in mind. But as I've grown older (and as I've grown up), I've seen that every lesson was not only packed with discipline and morality, but in each lesson was the vastness of your love for me. And I know that that love comes from God. Thank you for loving me with the forgiving, unyielding love of the Father. You have trained me in the ways I should go, and I will do my best to continue my journey through life along those ways.

Why God Made Mothers

Mothers Show Us the Value of Time

She gets up while it is still dark...
and her lamp does not go out at night.
PROVERBS 31:15, 18 NIV

Love is spelled T-I-M-E.

AUTHOR UNKNOWN

Acceptance and appreciation tell the child that
he or she is of tremendous worth.
And I can only express my acceptance and appreciation
through being affectionate—and available.

JOSH MCDOWELL

The best inheritance a parent can give his children
is a few minutes of his time each day.

O. A. BATTISTA

*There is so much to teach,
and the time goes by so fast.*

ERMA BOMBECK

If you are not willing to
make time for your children,
then every other piece of advice
you get is meaningless.
JOSH MCDOWELL

Why
God
Made
Mothers

Little drops of water, little grains of sand,
Make the mighty ocean and the beauteous land.
And the little moments, humble though they be,
Make the mighty ages of eternity.

JULIA CARNEY

*Time is given us to use
in view of eternity.*

AUTHOR UNKNOWN

Dost thou love life?
Then do not squander time,
for that is the stuff life is made of.

BENJAMIN FRANKLIN

Enjoy one another and take the time
to enjoy family life together.
Quality time is no substitute for quantity time.
Quantity time is quality time.

BILLY GRAHAM

Take time to think:
it is the course of power.
Take time to play:
it is the secret of perpetual youth.
Take time to read:
it is the fountain of wisdom.
Take time to laugh:
it is the music of the soul.
Take time to give:
it is too short a day to be selfish.

AUTHOR UNKNOWN

Lord,

thank You for the time You've given me with my family. It seems like you bless me by adding hours to the day so that I can be there for a special concert or the big game. Thank You for the moments when I am able to care for my family, even when I do not appreciate the tasks at hand—housework, carting kids around town, doctors' visits. . .the list is endless. For, in all these times, You allow me to be with my loved ones, and we are able to show each other how much we care. I know that the time we spend loving is well spent, because it is from You. In Your name, I pray. Amen.

What
I've Learned
from You. . .

She is energetic and strong, a hard worker. . .
She extends a helping hand to the poor
and opens her arms to the needy. . . . She has no fear of winter. . . .
When she speaks, her words are wise,
and kindness is the rule when she gives instructions.
PROVERBS 31:17, 20–21, 26 NLT

*Be the soul support
of your children.*

AUTHOR UNKNOWN

Sandwich every bit of criticism
between two layers of praise.
MARY KAY ASH

This is the day the LORD has made;
let us rejoice and be glad in it.
PSALM 118:24 NIV

*Why
God
Made
Mothers*

Praise your children openly; reprove them secretly.
W. CECIL

The greatest teacher is not experience;
it is example.
JOHN CROYLE

If you think you can do a thing or
think you can't do a thing, you're right.

HENRY FORD

Watch your thoughts;
they become words.
Watch your words;
they become actions.
Watch your actions;
they become habits.
Watch your habits;
they become character.
Watch your character;
it becomes your destiny.

FRANK OUTLAW

The greatest part of our happiness or misery
depends on our dispositions
and not on our circumstances.

MARTHA WASHINGTON

Take one thing with another,
and the world is a pretty good sort of a world,
and it is our duty to make the best of it,
and be thankful.

BENJAMIN FRANKLIN

Where there is great love there are miracles.

WILLA CATHER

In any project the important factor is your belief.
Without belief there can be no successful outcome.

WILLIAM JAMES

There are only two ways to live your life.
One is as though nothing is a miracle.
The other is as though everything is a miracle.

ALBERT EINSTEIN

Why
God
Made
Mothers

WHY *God* MADE *Mothers*

You have it easily in your power to increase
the sum total of this world's happiness now.
How? By giving a few words of sincere appreciation
to someone who is lonely or discouraged.
Perhaps you will forget tomorrow the kind words you say today,
but the recipient may cherish them over a lifetime.

DALE CARNEGIE

Kindness is a hard thing to give away;
it keeps coming back to the giver.

RALPH SCOTT

Don't hurry; don't worry.
You're only here for a short visit.
So be sure to stop and smell the flowers.

WALTER HAGEN

My parents taught me that I could do anything
I wanted and I have always believed it to be true.
Add a clear idea of what inspires you,
dedicate your energies to its pursuit,
and there is no knowing what you can achieve,
particularly if others are inspired by
your dream and offer their help.
PETE GOSS

*Why
God
Made
Mothers*

*If you carry your childhood with you,
you never become older.*
ABRAHAM SUTZKEVER

The older I get, the greater power I seem to have to help the world;
I am like a snowball—the further I am rolled, the more I gain.
SUSAN B. ANTHONY

Like kites without strings and butterfly wings,
my mother taught me to soar with my dreams.
WILLIAM H. MCMURRY III

WHY *God* MADE *Mothers*

If a child lives with encouragement,
he learns confidence.
If a child lives with praise,
he learns to appreciate.
If a child lives with fairness,
he learns justice.
If a child lives with security,
he learns to have faith.
If a child lives with approval,
he learns to like himself.
If a child lives with acceptance and friendship,
he learns to find love in the world.

DOROTHY NOLTE

Thanks, Mom

"There are many virtuous and capable women in the world,
but you surpass them all!"

PROVERBS 31:29 NLT

Though motherhood is
the most important of all the professions—
requiring more knowledge than
any other department in human affairs—
there was no attention given to preparation for this office.

ELIZABETH CADY STANTON

To My Mother

Because I feel that in heaven above
The angels, whispering one to another,
Can find among their burning terms of love,
None so devotional as that of "Mother,"
Therefore by that dear name I have long called you,
You who are more than mother to me.

EDGAR ALLAN POE

WHY *God* MADE *Mothers*

I will thank you, LORD,
in front of all the people.
I will sing your praises among the nations.
For your unfailing love is higher than the heavens.
Your faithfulness reaches to the clouds.
Be exalted, O God, above the highest heavens.
May your glory shine over all the earth.

PSALM 108:3–5 NLT

Her children stand and bless her.
Her husband praises her:
"There are many virtuous
and capable women in the world,
but you surpass them all!"
Reward her for all she has done.
Let her deeds publicly declare her praise.

PROVERBS 31:28–29, 31 NLT